The Book of
Intentions

The Book of
Intentions

The first step in creating a
more fulfilling life

Dianne Martin

BARNES & NOBLE BOOKS

NEW YORK

Published by MJF Books
Fine Communications
322 Eighth Avenue
New York, NY 10001

The Book of Intentions
LC Control Number 2003115176
ISBN 1-56731-657-3

Manufactured in the United States of America on acid-free paper ∞

MJF Books and the MJF colophon are trademarks of Fine Creative Media,
Inc.

VB   10 9   8   7   6   5   4   3   2   1

For Brian and Jack,
my two great loves

Contents

Introduction
Introduction

All of my life I have been taught (and have believed) that thought is powerful, that what we think influences what we bring into our experience, and that at all times we have the power to change our experience by changing our perception. I've also learned that love is omnipotent. It has the power to override negative thoughts, it has the power to perpetuate itself, and it has the power to create. Love is the strongest energy, and the strongest force.

Whenever we think, speak, or act, we inherently "intend" our experience at that moment. Each intention becomes a catalyst for experiences that interact with the thoughts, words, and actions of others. This collision and interaction of intentions can't help but profoundly affect our behavior, our environment, our communities, our world, our universe—and, therefore, our selves—on a very personal level.

Each intention is based on love—or it isn't. Either we live and cultivate an environment based on love—or we don't. And where there is no cognizant basis of love, chaos prevails.

The Book of Intentions was born out of my desire to raise my life to a higher level of experience. As I began writing "intentions" for myself, I thought about the fact that so many of us have common goals in all areas of our lives, such as work, play, love, family, community, and spirituality. It occurred to me that some sort of list could be a helpful tool to share with others; then I realized that a simple, straightforward book would be the answer. Not a lot of text, just intentions that others could work with from a personal point of view. But I didn't want the book to relax into shallow platitudes, I wanted to let it evolve into something that would dig deeper and promote real growth. And true growth is always at the spiritual level, not the material level—so the intentions are often connected to spirituality.

I offer this book to you as a resource—to help you anchor your thought in love, to help you keep your thought available solely for good, and to help you open your thought to all that may be true about the nature and purpose of your existence.

I invite you to take notice of your intentions, to take responsibility for your intentions, to take *control* of your intentions—and to do it with conviction. You will find, I expect—as I am finding—that in truly intending good you will think, speak, and act accordingly. You will bring more love and grace into your experience, and you will create a more harmonious, productive environment for yourself and for those around you.

As you intend a higher level of consciousness, you will begin to understand more clearly your personal mission for this life experience; and as you follow your spiritual mission, the elements of your life will fall into place and link together like a magnificent puzzle.

The Book of Intentions unfolds according to an evolution of thought and process. In chapter 1, I outline my ultimate intentions pertaining to spiritual growth. The successive chapters journey toward and through these goals, one at a time. They represent intention and contemplation regarding close relationships, behavior toward others in general, the planet, a higher power (which I refer to as God), healing, and purpose.

Recurring ideas are expressed throughout, in order to address them from a broad perspective as well as from within specific circumstances—and because certain spiritual lessons arise repeatedly, but in various aspects of our lives. For example, just when I think I've mastered fear, forgiveness, or compassion, I am presented with a more challenging opportunity to demonstrate my understanding. Admittedly, I have a long way yet to go.

I believe that many individuals share a number of these intentions, whether or not they've ever articulated them. I hope that you will recognize some of them as your own. I am sure that you, too, will find that one idea leads to another, and that you will continue to think of new ones along the way. I encourage you to write them down. Make notes. Make a commitment to do whatever it is that will help you, on a daily basis, pursue and achieve your spiritual goals.

If you come across something with which you don't agree or that you don't understand, move on to the next idea. Don't dwell on it unless you do so with the intention of understanding. I ask you to embrace only those ideas that resonate with your own sense of truth, good, and purpose.

I am eternally grateful to the spiritual trailblazers who continue to share their inspiration with the world, thereby inspiring others to achieve a higher expression of self.

I am grateful to you, the reader, for being part of this spiritual evolution.

The Book of
Intentions

I

Spiritual Understanding

Today I embark on a conscious spiritual journey. I acknowledge first my ultimate spiritual goals, knowing that in doing so I will be more likely to keep my thought focused, my intentions anchored, my vision clear.

I begin now.

I intend

to understand the power of intent

I intend

to comprehend the impact and ramifications
of thoughts, words, and actions

I intend

to use my thoughts, words, and actions
solely for good

I intend

to expect and desire only good,
for every individual,
and every situation

I intend

to maintain my life with gratitude and grace

to live in harmony and balance, and with purpose

I intend

to recognize and appreciate life's expressions—
plants, animals, and peoples—
in all their diversity

I intend

to radiate joy, happiness, and love
through my own inner peace
and warm regard for others

I intend

to comprehend that health, happiness, and empowerment
come from a spiritual source,
both infinite and eternal

I intend

to clear my consciousness of insecurity,
doubt, and fear

I intend

to acknowledge that I lack nothing,
and that I have always been, and will always be,
provided for

I intend

*to know that I am always guided
and protected*

I intend

*to be physically, mentally, and emotionally
unscarred by events, words, or ideas*

I intend

*to have a clear, unfailing understanding
of my own self-worth*

I intend

to redeem rather than condemn myself

to evaluate and correct my perceptions
rather than place judgment on the ideas or actions
of others

I intend

to respect and honor God's unconditional love
for everyone

to understand that love is the essence of God

I intend

to consider that existence is spiritual,
and so cannot be anything but complete and sound

to grasp the concept of spiritual perfection
and understand its natural expression
on the human level

to see that imperfection is a human illusion,
and that perfection is the underlying reality
waiting to be perceived

-

I intend

to comprehend my wholeness

to contemplate my spiritual unity with God,
and with all

I intend

to take spiritual steps as I am ready to take them

to progress from belief, to faith,
to spiritual understanding

to understand all there is to understand

I intend

to realize my creative purpose

I intend

to attune my thought to truth

2

Step by Step

I will now approach the details of my spiritual journey, step by step. I recognize that to reach toward a higher level of spiritual understanding is a natural but significant undertaking. I know that to avoid being overwhelmed, I must approach this goal thoughtfully and with balance.

I acknowledge that the challenge of spiritual growth is ultimately transcended by starting with the basic, and with the present moment. I will begin this personal process by elevating my everyday experience—knowing that there are countless opportunities to lift my thought a little higher, to act and interact in a constructive manner, and to appreciate the abundance and beauty of life.

I see that moment by moment, I develop a daily ritual, and year by year, that ritual evolves into a personal rhythm of life. I know that it is up to me to actively compose my life's rhythm and to fully realize its potential.

I will begin, today, to raise my thought, action, intention, and expectation to a higher, more inspiring, rhythm of purpose.

I intend

to begin each day by inviting spiritual growth

I intend

*to incorporate that which I learn spiritually
into my daily life and work*

I intend

to approach my tasks responsibly,
efficiently, and with love,
so that I may accomplish them effectively
and without the stress of disorganization,
dread, or resentment

to work in the moment,
focusing on the project and process at hand

I intend

*to understand that I slow my progress
if I think too much of the past or the future,
for the only relevant moment of this life's purpose
is now*

I intend

*to release every memory that evokes pain,
sadness, resentment, or anger*

to perceive the lessons of past mistakes

*to heal and release all regrets and self-condemnation,
for they are no longer of use to me,
and only delay the greater story of my life*

I intend

*to remain flexible regarding what I want
or think I need*

*to examine the relationship between my desires
and my motives*

*to look forward to the next step, turn, or
unexpected twist in my life,
accepting new challenges as fresh opportunities to learn*

*to regard each major turning point, whether easy or difficult,
as a gateway to the next level of experience*

I intend

to let myself trust the process of spiritual development

to understand that finding inner peace is a personal journey

I intend

to approach life with humor, passion, and purpose

*to take time to garden, to cook, to dance,
to picnic, to learn, and to play*

*to share these personal pleasures with my loved ones,
from all parts of my life*

*to take extraordinary pleasure
in ordinary moments of fun*

I intend

to make decisions consciously,
with wisdom and grace

to move forward,
discovering and manifesting my life
in a fresh, spontaneous, and true light

to expect the natural providence
of serendipitous discoveries and events

to embrace each new day and give thanks
for its wealth of possibilities

I intend

to acknowledge all the good in my life
and to gratefully understand and accept its richness
and abundance

to thank God for such loving attention

I intend

to resist idolizing another person,
or thinking of anyone as more admirable,
more important, or more special than I

to appreciate my own unique combination of characteristics

I intend

to perceive myself as I am:
a perfect reflection of a perfect creator

to understand that expressing divine perfection
is not accomplished by striving for human perfection—
but is my very essence

to see that human flaws have no true basis,
and no true substance

I intend

to treat myself and others with dignity

*to remember that true radiance is spiritual,
and that true spirituality is radiant*

I intend

to attain relaxation and inspiration naturally

to use physical exercise and activity
to express grace, joy,
and life

to tend body and mind with love and respect

I intend

to recognize the value of education

*to recognize that there are countless avenues
for cultivating knowledge and gaining insight,
and that everyone I meet has wisdom to impart*

*to welcome new acquaintances and activities,
knowing that they will enrich my experience
and broaden my understanding*

I intend

to renew my sense of adventure

to take joy in mastering new skills
and overcoming old fears

I intend

to see all thought of destruction, or prophecy of doom,
as the antithesis of creation,
and therefore the antithesis of truth

I intend

to expand my vision and deepen my insight

to grasp the truth by exploring,
experiencing, and practicing it on my own

I intend

to remember that love is the key to spiritual understanding

*to anchor the intention of love in my thought
and in my heart*

I intend

to live my life in a way that inspires others
to live theirs to their greatest potential

I intend

to welcome the responsibility of living a life
based on clear intent

3

Family and Friends

I will now turn my attention to the most important people in my life, as I know that tremendous spiritual growth comes from the closest, dearest—and often most challenging—relationships.

I recognize that it is my family members and closest friends who support me in my greatest abundance and meekest poverty, in my highest achievements and most abject failures. And I acknowledge that, with each relationship, I continue to learn more about compassion, forgiveness, love, and loyalty.

I will examine my life and recognize how I can strengthen my relationships—how I can reclaim for them their freshness, vitality, and special place in my world. I will see that their spark never fades, and their value never diminishes.

I will tend to my family and friends more carefully, allowing each relationship to develop lovingly, fully, and brilliantly.

I will remember that we have important spiritual work to do, together.

I intend

to work toward a wholly supportive,
cooperative, and loving interaction
with my family and friends

I intend

to react and interact with compassion,
warmth, and joy

I intend

to treasure my family and friends

*to show them my attention, my appreciation,
my gratitude*

to do it now, not "later"

I intend

to give a high priority to time with my family and friends

to know them and care for them
on a more personal and thoughtful level

to be responsive to their hopes, fears,
aspirations, and needs

to acknowledge that their presence in my life
is a blessing

I intend

*to avoid labeling the characteristics and idiosyncrasies
of my family and friends*

*to see how labels, even when used with affection,
tend to limit my perceptions of others*

*to allow my family and friends
to express themselves in new ways,
to be willing to see them in a different light,
and to see their endless potential*

to let them make their own decisions

*to project only nurturing thoughts
and the highest expectation
for their happiness and success*

I intend

to resist criticizing or condemning
the thoughts, words, actions, and choices
of my family, my friends, and myself

to recognize the difference
between thoughtful debate and intolerance,
between advocacy and control

to strive for discernment

I intend

to forgive my loved ones, and myself

to comprehend that it is not anyone's place
to withhold forgiveness of anyone else

to acknowledge that when I withhold
forgiveness from others, I make it impossible
to forgive myself—and that in each instance
my own spiritual progress is further impeded

I intend

to appreciate the natural purity and innocence
of my child

to foster my child's uncensored, exuberant
expression of love, joy, wisdom, creativity,
curiosity, and activity

to let my child learn and grow,
without pressure, without comparison,
without criticism, and without fear

to be a constant, but not intrusive, support
for my child

to let my child teach me about life,
and to let myself be amazed

to nurture and love my child unconditionally

I intend

to cherish the love and company of my partner,
and appreciate the depth of our relationship

to ensure that my partner, my dearest friend,
feels valued, respected, supported, loved, and desired

to know that by living and learning together in love,
we continue our affinity and our evolution
as kindred sparks of Spirit

to nurture and love my partner unconditionally

I intend

to honor sex as a unique commitment,
and to enjoy it as an expression
of unequalled love, intimacy, and trust

I intend

*to recognize that sensuality evokes an ironic
craving for the intangible and for the spiritual*

*to see how anything good that I can
experience with my physical senses—
no matter how intense, and how pleasurable—
has a higher, spiritual counterpart
that is even more profound*

*to understand that it is the spiritual aspect of
good experience—its essence—
that I desire*

I intend

to value relationships outside of my bond with my partner—
and to allow my partner to do the same

to ensure that my connections to others do not compromise,
on any level,
the integrity of my relationship with my partner

I intend

to stay in regular contact with family and friends,
and take the time and care to develop
full and loving relationships with them

to let family and friends move in and out of my life as they need to,
with the assurance that they are always welcome

to embrace and foster lifelong connections

I intend

to know that however much I cherish my partner,
my child, my family, and my friends,
I must let go of counterproductive emotional bonds

to see that in order to love and support each other unconditionally,
we must be anchored to spirituality
and not to each other's expectations,
thoughts, words, actions, or judgments

I intend

to appreciate the spiritual essence and underlying potential
of kinship, even among strangers

to perceive and acknowledge sincere gestures
of love and affection that otherwise
may be misread or overlooked

I intend

to freely give whatever assistance I can,
to whomever needs it

to let my favors be favors, and gifts be gifts—
without expecting something in return
or instilling a sense of debt

to graciously, as well as gratefully,
accept gifts, favors, and assistance—
understanding that others find joy in being of service,
just as I do

I intend

to accept that I am responsible for my own
sense of peace, happiness, and emotional security

to give my family and friends room to develop spiritually,
knowing that we can express mutual respect and consideration
without stifling one another

to understand that relationships are meant to be enriching,
not confining

I intend

to understand that trust is a gift of unconditional love,
given without fear of violation
or threat of repossession

to recognize that trust is an offering to hold dear

I intend

to love unconditionally my partner, my child, my family, and my friends

I intend

to remember that spiritual heritage
does not come from mortal parents,
and that we are all family through God

4

Social Grace

I will now look to social grace as a rung high on the ladder of spiritual growth, and begin correcting behavior that doesn't meet my standard of ethics, integrity, duty, compassion, and love.

I will perceive grace as a divine, selfless love projected by God—through each of us, to our surroundings—and then reflected back, with the lesson being that we are inextricably connected: We are one. I will understand that if I could look into a large enough mirror, I would see not only myself, but the world, its universe, and other universes—and will know that everyone in this vast existence is part of my reflection, and I am part of theirs. In the same sense, if I were to pick up a piece of a broken mirror, I would still see myself; and though I wouldn't be able to see my entire physical image, nor my spiritual identity, I'd know that both existed as part of me in this human experience.

In reflecting grace, I will now make conscious decisions to demonstrate my highest understanding of love, God, and self, in every respect, at any time, in any place, under any circumstance.

Through grace, I will lovingly support the whole.

I intend

to extend love and friendship to all

to appreciate the diverse characteristics of others
for their uniqueness, for their honest expression
and for their distinct contribution to the world

to let others express spirit unstifled

to provide an environment in which others feel welcome
and comfortable

I intend

to recognize the inherent beauty of each person I meet

*to appreciate how each of us is gifted
with a uniquely appealing image of size,
shape, age, color, and gender*

I intend

to accept that we are all ideas of God—
expressions of life, love, joy, beauty, truth, and intelligence—
and as such, God does not identify us
by race, religion, gender, age, class, or background

to understand that, as reflections of God,
we cannot be intended to treat each other
with anything but respect, love, and compassion

to know that each of us exists to express and enjoy love

I intend

to nurture excellence in activities
that are guided by good

to be proud of and inspired by those
who successfully exhibit their highest sense of self

to encourage others to be pleased with their accomplishments,
and welcome them to share their expertise

to rejoice in the prosperity of others

to let others shine

I intend

to reconsider my heroes

to celebrate those who devote their lives
in service to others for the purpose of good

to value those who work with dedication,
creativity, and integrity

to learn from those who maintain inner peace
regardless of circumstance

I intend

to exhibit joy without embarrassment or self-consciousness

*to evince the admirable qualities I see in others
without copying their personal mannerisms*

*to recognize and rectify my behavioral weaknesses
rather than accept them as intrinsic to my identity*

*to perceive life lessons through intuition when possible—
and through experience when necessary*

I intend

to fulfill my responsibilities

to commit only when I can honor the commitment

to communicate clearly

to say no when necessary

to find balance, comfort, and freedom in responsibility

I intend

to disallow the possibility of hurting another individual,
consciously or unconsciously

to correct harm done to another

to help mend weakened bridges,
whether they are mine or someone else's

I intend

to rid myself of pettiness and insecurity

to recognize when my apology is due

to have the grace to sincerely admit,
"You're right," "I'm wrong," and "I'm sorry"

to resist assigning or implying blame

to acknowledge that I will be presented with opportunities
to learn forgiveness and humility
until each is understood

I intend

to take time for thoughtful communication

*to acknowledge that refusing to communicate
is more insidious than agreed disagreement*

*to resolve conflict as smoothly as possible,
to release it, and to move on
with a heightened understanding of grace*

I intend

to see the highest potential in,
and expect the highest experience for,
every child, woman, and man

to think toward the health, happiness, and well-being of others—
rather than indulging in speculation
regarding their accidents, mistakes, or misfortunes

to question any instance in which my love and support for another
are not absolute and implicit

I intend

to cherish the innocence, purity, joy, wisdom,
expression, and true incorruptibility of children

to remember that children benefit immensely
if they have even one person
who offers them a stable sense of love and support

to encourage children in their education,
endeavors, and aspirations—
to nurture their responsibility, confidence, ingenuity,
and understanding of God's unconditional love

to acknowledge that adults, too, need at least one person
whom they can trust for love, support, and encouragement

I intend

to honor the spiritual paths of others

to resist imposing on others my own values or beliefs

to perceive and respect the privacy,
confidentiality, and boundaries of others

to love, without reservation, judgment, or prejudice

to recognize the innocence that we all retain
as children of God

I intend

to welcome contact with people of diverse
backgrounds, interests, and experience

to appreciate that having contrasting personalities
within one family or group
provides opportunities for interaction among those
whose spheres would not ordinarily intersect

to recognize that imposed bonds,
whether through relationships or circumstances,
serve to promote compassion and respect—
and to dispel judgment, condemnation, and ostracization—
toward those whom we might not ordinarily accept

to see how, as members of God's family,
we cannot truly have conflicting identities

I intend

to disregard a damaged reputation
in light of present intent and action

to recognize that "reputation" implies
judgment and labeling by others

to comprehend that spiritual law
deems the judgment of others
inappropriate and unjust

I intend

to understand that if I regard someone as being less than perfect,
I indulge the concept of imperfection
and hinder my own spiritual growth

to respect that we each have our own lessons,
successes, and apparent failures to experience
and grow from

to remember that each of us is living our life
chapter by chapter, scene by scene,
and that we each have our own story

to see my judgment or pity of others as a reminder
that I have plenty of spiritual room to grow

I intend

to perceive the lessons of tragedy on a spiritual level,
but never relinquish my role as a humanitarian

to see that my action or inaction regarding the suffering of others
indicates the depth of my compassion

to understand that passivity in the face of atrocity
is never justified

I intend

to effect change for good through whatever means
are appropriate for me

to pray before tragedy has an opportunity to occur,
rather than waiting until it has happened

I intend

*to consider my true, purposeful link to those I encounter,
and to see that we have a greater reason for meeting
than to accomplish mere human tasks*

*to trust spiritual direction, as well as human interaction,
in order to discover and fulfill the purpose of our meeting*

I intend

to anchor my thought in love when thinking of others

to answer spiritual calls for help

to know God is already guiding me

to remember to listen for that guidance

5

Planet Earth

I will now consider my environment—the physical setting into which I was born—and its spiritual significance.

I recognize the Earth context as a teaching ground within the greater cosmos, and the cosmos as an expanded concept of physical existence—and I know that the cosmos exists, as all concepts do, within the realm of an ultimate consciousness. I see that it is my thought, not my environment, that shapes me. It is my expectation, reaction, and intention that ripple through my experience, creating a world.

I will begin now to absorb the beauty of Earth's features—its shape, size, landscape, and bodies of water—and to truly appreciate its myriad peoples, cultures, creatures, and expressions of life. I will begin now to work cooperatively and compassionately on Earth, to help its communities thrive, and to reap respectfully its gifts of shelter, sustenance, and inspiration.

I will appreciate Earth for the spectacular home it is, experience and acknowledge its gifts, nurture it with attentive care, and visualize it as healthy and whole, with a beautiful future.

I will see how Earth expresses creation—how Earth expresses God.

I intend

to regard my life on Earth as an extraordinary gift

I intend

to notice everyday objects and people
with the fresh curiosity and appreciation of a child

I intend

*to experience the brilliance, beauty, and joy of life
expressed through the symphony of colors, sounds, flavors,
images, ideas, aromas, sensations, words, and possibilities
offered to me on a daily basis*

I intend

to respect Earth and foster its growth

to tend to all expressions of life with love

to treasure each form of nature
as an individual brush stroke of Spirit

I intend

to have reverence for all peoples, animals, and plants,
and for the earth I walk on

to recognize that plants, animals, Earth, and the universe
operate under the same spiritual truths as we do,
because all exist within the spiritual consciousness of God

to see that all forms of life, including plants and animals,
respond to love as their supreme influence

to consider how a thriving environment
contributes to the richness of my experience

I intend

to cherish each season for its distinct characteristics
and penetrating symbolism

I intend

to value the air, earth, fire, and water

to take delight in the rain, snow, grass, soil,
rock, sand, and sun

to marvel at and respect the mountains,
forests, jungles, beaches, oceans, deserts,
skies, rolling hills, and wide open country,
and the wonderful creatures
that call each of these places their home

I intend

to regard nature's activity as an expression,
rather than a threat of annihilation

to comprehend and fully appreciate
that all of nature and humanity are expressions of God,
and that they operate within and according to
God's harmonious principle of life

I intend

to rejoice in the energy of the dawn,
savor the stillness of dusk,
and accept both events
as invitations for contemplation

to imagine, at sunrise,
the realm of joyous possibilities for the day,
and to expect only a perfect unfolding

to reflect, at sunset, on what I have learned,
and to be grateful for the gifts of the day

to set my expectation for tomorrow to bring
an even more beautiful experience and understanding

I intend

to let the stars' disappearance with the dawn
remind me that just because I can't see, hear,
taste, feel, or otherwise perceive something,
it doesn't mean that it isn't there

I intend

to consider the spiritual significance of light

I intend

to speculate on the allegorical purpose and placement
of the bright golden sphere we call the sun

to muse on the symbolic import of the moon,
a light that stays with us through the night,
beckoning us beyond this Earth experience

I intend

to explore the world's tapestry of race, creed, and culture

I intend

to reappraise my values

to resist forming an attachment to material possessions

to periodically clean house of obsolete values
and extraneous items

to notice how my spiritual awareness increases
when I shift my attention toward nature
and away from a manufactured environment

I intend

to maintain an awareness of world activities

*to respond to global events with an acknowledgment
of God's universal presence—
therefore acknowledging, also, the inherent presence
of stability, harmony, and peace*

I intend

to observe my world, absorb its lessons,
and appreciate its place in the bigger picture of existence

to understand that the human experience
is only part of a greater life story

to consider that life is about spiritual evolution,
not about the details of human history

I intend

to assist my community by participating
in its maintenance, growth, and well-being

to promote supportive relationships
between communities and cultures

to bolster a greater sense of world community,
and help diminish fear and its resulting selfishness

to understand the magnificent potential of a world community
consciously operating with the intention of love

I intend

to go where I am impelled to go,
to interact with others along the way,
and to gain insight via the exchange

to convey that which is helpful
to the appropriate people at the appropriate time

to communicate clearly for the purpose of good,
unhindered by differences of culture, language, politics, or religion

to carry within me the concept of home,
and to share with others the warm familiarity of a family

I intend

*to welcome the uninhibited ideas of children
and the quixotic philosophies of each new generation—*

*to appreciate them as indicators of the possible,
and reminders of the ideal*

I intend

to envision only ideas, words, and events of the highest good flourishing on planet Earth

6

The Power That Is

I will now contemplate spirituality itself, and consider the power—the source and law of life—I call God.

I acknowledge that the more I ponder and affirm the truths I perceive about God, the easier it will be to deny the reality of anything unlike God. For example, I know that in God's consciousness—which is absolute, constant, harmonious, and perfect—there is no place for fear.

I see that to have a clear understanding of God's love, presence, and protection, is to know an unparalleled sense of peace. I recognize this clarity as not only comforting, but as a necessary foundation for all of my experience. It is a spiritual anchor in an otherwise shifting and uncer-tain time.

I realize that it is impossible to study spirituality mean-ingfully without learning about God. And I know that as

I gradually grasp more about God, I will discover more about myself.

I know that my highest, most beautiful, most spiritual concept of God will always be the most accurate approximation of what God is.

I will begin now to explore the nature of God, and learn how I, a creation of God, reflect God's essence.

I intend

to discover that which lies beyond the periphery of mortal existence

to discern the spiritual aspect and reality of life

to understand God as principle, as truth, as the law of life

I intend

to acknowledge that "God" is one name for the power of life,
and that others may use a different name

to let others discover and demonstrate
their own understanding of God,
in their own way

I intend

to appreciate those who are dedicated to the sciences—
for their desire to probe, to ascertain, to educate,
and to aid in the progression of humankind

to consider that science exists as a human concept
within a human context

to delve beyond physics and the human context,
into metaphysics

to recognize science and technology
as mere scribblings on the chalkboard of Mind

I intend

to perceive the reality of intrinsic harmony and order

to accept that God does not send evil, punishment, or tragedy

to know I can never fall out of God's unchanging perfection
and constant protection

I intend

to recognize that both lack of control,
and fear of losing control,
hold important spiritual lessons

to recognize that excessive desires, cravings,
obsessions, addictions, and unproductive habits
are simply symptoms of unbalanced spiritual understanding,
evidenced by a distorted sense of need

I intend

to fathom that I carry within me the ability
to abolish fear and break the illusion of danger,
regardless of the situation

to see degradation as a dark and destructive act
which can be overcome through a higher understanding of self,
and a deeper understanding of identity

to recognize that which some identify as a dark power
is actually an obstruction of light,
casting a dark experience

to know that it is up to me to let in the light

I intend

to comprehend the power of thought,
the power of belief,
the power of understanding,
and the power of love

to know that there is nothing more powerful than love

I intend

to understand that there is only one mind—
one consciousness, one God—
and only one soul

to recognize that an idea from God
is assimilated readily
and needn't be explained or translated

to discern between thoughts from God
and human will

to respect human authority as necessary,
but to understand there can be no higher authority than God

I intend

to know that we are each connected to a higher source,
and that none of us needs an intermediary
to communicate with that source

I intend

to anticipate divine support
and to recognize divine supply

to rejoice in the beauty, joy, creativity,
expression, and grace of God

to consider that God—Spirit—is substance and soul

to thank God, daily, for guidance and gifts proffered

I intend

to resist attributing power to humans

to know instead that those who have
positions of apparent control
are governed by God

to expect and affirm that all express God
through skill, integrity, and wisdom

I intend

to see how personal will, loss of discernment, and fear
lead us into conflict, confusion and, ultimately,
into a compromise of our highest values

to bear in mind that it is up to me, not God,
to solve my human problems,
do my spiritual homework, and learn my life lessons—
but that God is always there,
leading me through these challenges

I intend

to attune my ear to God,
and learn to recognize God's voice and direction

to have the courage to forge ahead into the unknown,
when guided to do so

to be undaunted

I intend

to cherish my attunement to peace,
and use it as a form of prayer

to recognize that God's love is unconditional,
and that it embraces each one of us

to imagine the deeply intense love of a parent for a child—
and know that God's love for me is even greater than that

to understand that God is love, and love is God

I intend

*to monitor what I allow to possess my thoughts
and influence my words, actions, and desires*

I intend

to see that it is purity of thought
that gives me spiritual clarity

to keep my thought pure by admitting only
what is anchored in my highest, purest understanding of love,
and my highest, purest understanding of God's perfection

to see, as I progress
from belief, to faith, to spiritual understanding,
that I gain an absolute understanding of God's power

to hold to that understanding with unshakeable conviction

I intend

to perceive miracles as reminders from God
that human and physical laws are not absolute,
that human reality is not as solid as it seems to be,
and that true reality is not determined by human experience

to appreciate these truly natural events
as hints of a greater presence,
and as a reminder that we are spiritual

I intend

to understand that God is everywhere

I intend

to remain alert solely to good, even while sleeping

*to exercise the option to accept or reject
information and images*

*to convey and accept only those thoughts and images
that are based on the intention of love*

I intend

to comprehend that I exist in the consciousness of God—
that I am a point of consciousness in mind,
a spiritual idea of God

to recognize that others, too, are spiritual ideas of God

to see that if something seems to happen or exist
that is not of God, it is merely a dream,
an illusory inversion of what is good and true

to break the illusion of the dream—
and see that if something wouldn't exist
in God's consciousness, it doesn't really exist

to wake up and know that God is

7

Natural Instinct

I will now use my spiritual understanding to transcend daily challenges, personal struggles, and seemingly unfair predicaments. I will acknowledge turmoil as an unnatural state, anxiety as a cultivated reflex. I will see healing as my true natural instinct.

I know that healing is a result of the moments I take to remind myself of my spiritual identity and purpose, regardless of where I am or what I am doing. I recognize that each challenge—whether physical, mental, emotional, or social—can draw me into a maelstrom of fear and frustration only if I give my consent. I realize that it is up to me to keep watch, detecting and healing unrest before it manifests itself further in my life. It is up to me to exercise my spiritual resiliency.

I intend to rediscover my spiritual resiliency by responding to all forms of fear with love—love of others, of the common good, of God, of self, and of life's adventure. I will reclaim my true natural instinct—accepting only ideas that promote healthy interaction and that affirm the beauty and incorruptibility of life.

I will begin now to remember healing as my instinctive, preventive, and progressive way of being.

I intend

to resist giving mental energy to disease, discord, and dislike

*to recognize that what I focus on in fear and judgment
is what I draw into my experience to overcome*

to heal the fear underlying each problem or concern that arises

*to know that my healings and personal points of progress
result in layers of understanding and a depth of experience,
which enable me to reach and support others*

I intend

to ponder the purpose of religion,
appreciate its constant invitation,
give thanks for its healing role,
and recognize its spiritual essence

to appreciate religious structures as
ubiquitous reminders of God's presence—
and to respect that the ritual of religion provides,
for many, a special time to talk with God

to value spiritual gathering places,
and feel the potential magnitude of a shared consciousness
concentrating on love and intending good

to see individual study and community congregation
as natural instincts that contribute
to the understanding and celebration of God

I intend

to refine my spiritual instinct through prayer

to use prayer as a time to remind myself
of the spiritual truths I know about myself, about others,
about life, love, and the nature of God—
and to correct any thoughts, words, actions, and reactions
that are not based on these truths

to use prayer as a time to completely clear my thought
and actively listen

to remember that I can pray anywhere,
at any time, in any circumstance

I intend

to release the grip of financial worries, career concerns,
and any other feelings of personal instability and vulnerability—
and trust that everything I need, including protection,
will be provided as I need it

to act responsibly, but resist the temptation
to overplan my life or shield my experience

to anticipate that each day will provide new insight,
new opportunities for growth, and new ways to surprise me
with resolution, abundance, and direction

I intend

to resist being devastated by another's absence

to know that whoever was, still is;
and that we carry within us our connection
to each other, to life, and to God

to understand that love, joy, and expression
cannot be extinguished

to let myself grieve, and to let grief heal

I intend

to see that relationship problems are rooted in fear,
and that they can be healed through love
and a desire for resolution

to heal my fear without blaming someone else

to alleviate another's fear by conveying
compassion, consideration, and respect
in all levels of interaction

to recognize my own value
and see that I don't need to prove myself,
don't need to demand attention,
and don't need to struggle
for power or control

I intend

to heal any personal sense of envy, jealousy,
greed, or emotional insecurity

to see that nothing and no one else
can make me more successful, more confident, more loved,
more whole, more satisfied, or more secure

to recognize my inherent beauty, prosperity,
wholeness, and worth

to regard the compulsion to obtain material assets,
social status, or affection
as an attempt to possess self-respect and self-love

I intend

to comprehend that no one part of my body
is any less whole than another

to heal indications of disease, distress, injury, and age
by recognizing that they manifest through fear
and a belief in mortality

to resist focusing on physical disease and injury,
and to visualize, instead, my spiritual perfection

to bring the human picture into alignment
with its flawless spiritual reality

to understand that challenges are opportunities for spiritual growth,
and are never sent as punishments from God

I intend

to acknowledge that maintaining my body as a machine—
as separate from God—
will allow me to feel vulnerable to its mortal malfunctions

to know that to ignore, abuse, or disrespect my physical body
will bring spiritual challenges

to understand how,
through excessive attention or blatant disregard,
I unwittingly give control to the concept of matter
rather than to mind

I intend

to recognize signs of age as illusions

to see that, regarding age, numbers have
vastly different meanings to different individuals—
and are ultimately meaningless

to resist conforming my identity
to the time-related expectations of others

to embark on each new phase of life
with uncircumscribed anticipation

I intend

to grasp that any sense of restriction
represents a human story
rather than a spiritual reality

to see that my real self is greater than any story it creates
and is always inherently agile, intelligent, and whole

to comprehend that the one consciousness,
the one mind, cannot deteriorate

to know that I am of divine energy,
and therefore cannot malfunction, break, decay,
or die

to understand that God is my life and sustenance,
and that God, the principle of life, cannot end

I intend

to heal depression and feelings of futility, failure, and self-doubt
by knowing that I have been given a distinct means
of expressing God,
that I am not to measure myself against others,
and that I have within me the natural desire, energy, and ability
to discover and fulfill my own special purpose

to heal shame by realigning my identity with God,
and rehabilitating my sense of purpose

to heal despair by listening for guidance
and accepting that I am loved by God

to help those in despair find joy
through discovering their own value and purpose

I intend

to heal painful memories by recognizing
that each challenging event is an indication
that I am ready to take a big leap spiritually

to let my rage subside, and allow room for healing

to understand that it is impossible
for a creation of God to be intrinsically evil

to let God's love lead me through every dark episode

I intend

to help heal injury to my community
by supporting its recovery and vitality

to help heal political and governmental disease
by letting go of my own self-righteousness, fear,
and accusation of others

to see that we are governed and provided for by God,
not by fellow human beings

to pray not for my favorite candidate to take office,
but for wisdom to discern the most appropriate person
for a particular position at a particular time

I intend

to support public officials in their desire
to be guided by wisdom and integrity—
and to know that it is possible for them to be effective
in their good intentions

to know that public personalities are advised and protected by God

I intend

to heal prejudice and hatred by dispelling fear of loss—
loss of control, freedom, and autonomy;
loss of material possessions and personal affections;
loss of identity, self-esteem, and respect;
loss of individual achievement and public success

to see that my dislike or distrust of someone
is always born of fear—
and that such fear is my responsibility to heal

to understand that there is no danger in sharing insight,
or threat in working together for good

to remember that there is one mind,
helping us to work cooperatively and harmoniously

I intend

to express wisdom and clarity of thought
when confronted with a crisis

to heal the fear of personal responsibility

to let my highest sense of integrity,
and an understanding of spiritual sovereignty,
counsel me in all difficult decisions

to resist letting fear cause me to doubt
what I know to be true about myself, about others,
and about God

to regard God as my confidant and mentor

I intend

to help heal situations of abuse and dependency

to see that I cannot truly assist the healing of abuse
if I am condoning, tolerating, or somehow supporting abuse myself

to recognize that I am trapped spiritually
if I am abusing individuals, people, animals,
substances, or circumstances

to help others break the familial link,
and social chain, of abuse and dependency

I intend

to take responsibility for the mental environment
to which I expose myself and others

to reject any thought or image
regarding myself or others
that I do not desire to have manifested
in my body or in my experience

to refine my reflexes by removing anger,
angst, apathy, arrogance, criticism,
defensiveness, irritability, moodiness,
resentment, smugness, and fear
from my realm of possibilities

I intend

to see the implications and manifestations
of labeling myself as "sensitive"

to recognize how the word "sensitive" implies
emotional, mental, or physical vulnerability

to be, instead, compassionate, perceptive, and resilient

to affirm that nothing can scar a spiritual being—
physically, emotionally, psychologically, or psychically

to release mental baggage and other traces of injury,
and invite love to heal, instinctively,
every facet of my life

to understand that, in the consciousness of God,
there is truly nothing that needs to be healed

8

Creative Purpose

I will now contemplate my creative purpose. I will begin by looking to the arts, for whenever I witness the pure and passionate expression of art, I know that I am in the presence of divine inspiration being realized—and I am reminded of what it is to be so finely attuned to one's own creative purpose.

I know that, regardless of my vocation, I, too, have a creative purpose, and that I am continually given opportunities to share that expression on a conscious and intentional level. I see that when I feel truly inspired to pursue a particular path, or share a specific skill, I am being divinely directed. I consider inspiration to be my creative compass, giving me guidance to—and through—the path of my purpose. I recognize that I, too, have a pure passion, a clear vision, and a desire, born from inspiration, to affect others in a powerful, productive way. I acknowledge that if I have the courage to follow inspiration, I will be able to help others to do the same.

I will assert a renewed appreciation for artists and others who share themselves on such a deeply personal level. I will recognize their work as a reminder to express myself creatively, and to be equally dedicated.

I will begin now to explore and fulfill my own creative purpose.

I intend

to imagine that we are God's artistic expression

to consider that we are intended to express creativity

to see how our expressions of creativity
enrich the life of the whole—
and reflect the whole of life

I intend

to contemplate the reason that all cultures
have felt impelled to sing, to dance, to draw—
to express themselves creatively

to regard spiritual and cultural roots
as beautifully unique, personal settings
from which a story begins

to recognize that each of us tells a story
in the way that we live our lives

I intend

to appreciate the arts as God's gift of candid, insightful expression

to respect the artist's bold and vulnerable use of personal expression
to address the complex needs of a broad audience

I intend

to consider that art enables me to interpret my world
from an extended dimension

to appreciate the power of art to draw me in,
and to allow me to discover its message from within its form,
from my own perspective

to accept the invitation proffered by art
to examine life from a new angle—
a fresh vantage point
from which I can expand my awareness,
gain a greater understanding of others,
formulate and solidify my values,
and develop my own creative purpose

I intend

to let music resonate through the layers of my being,
and open me to a higher level of awareness

to let dance capture me with its vitality, elegance, and passion

to acknowledge the emotional and spiritual yearning
evoked by music and dance

to muse over the artist's ability
to render my innermost thoughts

I intend

to be grateful for a world abundant with music,
dance, theater, film, sculpture, painting, poetry, prose,
storytelling, and public forums for sharing ideas and emotions

to recognize the myriad forms of art
as distinct and profound methods of communication

I intend

to see that talent is inspiration expressed,
a gift cherished

to show gratitude for those
who follow their inspiration long and far enough
to share their gift with the rest of the world

to send messages of love, appreciation, and encouragement
to those who would not know otherwise
that they have touched me with their work

I intend

to respect heartfelt sentiment
as well as intellectual and esoteric analysis

to understand that all perceptions of art,
and all sincere attempts to communicate through art,
are valid

to see that no expression of creativity
can be analyzed objectively

to remember that though I may not be touched
by the work of another,
others may be profoundly affected

to reject the idea that art should affect everyone equally

I intend

to remember that fame and fortune are not universal goals,
and that just as we each have our own story,
we each have individual routes
by which we discover and express purpose

to know that all expressions are gifts,
none less significant than another,
and that fulfillment of divine purpose,
executed with love and dedication,
is art in its purest form

I intend

to understand and acknowledge
that inspiration comes from a higher source
and does not originate in a physical body

to recognize that ideas present themselves to us
because we each have a unique perspective, vision,
and means of communicating them to others

to let creativity flow freely through me
and to honor inspiration graciously and gratefully to completion

I intend

to see that when art is used to blame rather than enlighten,
to injure rather than heal, or corrupt rather than purify,
it is merely an announcement of the artist's personal conflicts
and should be treated with compassion

I intend

to develop my understanding and expression of spirit

to let my forms of expression be shaped and guided
by the highest level of consciousness,
for the highest good

to relinquish those characteristics that stifle joy, grace, or love—
or otherwise obstruct the flow of divine energy

to have clarity of purpose and boundless vision

I intend

to monitor my intent in all forms of my expression,
and to remain steadfast in those endeavors
that best express my sense of purpose

to maintain integrity,
regardless of the favorable or unfavorable responses of others

to remember that it is possible to be flexible in form
without compromising in substance

I intend

to let spirit guide my decisions—
even if it means taking risks

I intend

to release the notion that I need to impress others

to remember that the most effective work
is created through inspiration and dedication,
that it does not fit a mold,
and that, like character, it comes from within
and speaks to others through a new voice

to understand that contrived uniqueness lacks emotion,
substance, integrity, and depth

to accept that my work is meant to reach particular individuals,
and that others will be reached through alternative avenues

I intend

to accomplish my work as necessary,
to overcome obstacles with grace,
and to execute my endeavors to their greatest potential

to rely on a higher source of wisdom and illumination
to lead me when I feel lost or discouraged

to use moments of total silence
as opportunities to listen

I intend

to comprehend that the success of others
does not threaten my own accomplishments or self-worth

to remember that another's achievements are not intended for me,
and that I have my own achievements to make

to understand that all my needs are met
and will continue to be met
if I trust the path I am being guided to take

to recognize opportunities and to use them wisely

I intend

to appreciate the arts for capturing our imagination,
sparking thoughtful discussion,
and igniting the creative impulse

to value, support, and celebrate teachers,
for selflessly devoting their lives
to the development, progress, and success of others

to appreciate all who work with the intention
of encouraging, nurturing, and inspiring others

to honor all who give selflessly of their time,
energy, money, expertise, or spirit
for the sake of helping others

I intend

to see how we each express God
in a uniquely beautiful, brilliant, and necessary way,
and know that no one else can replace that expression

to consciously, intentionally, act on inspiration,
and realize my own creative purpose

I intend

to understand that it is never too late to discover purpose,
it is never too late to strive for excellence,
it is never too late to begin

to begin now

Epilogue

Epilogue

Every day, I come a little bit closer to a true understanding of how my spiritual development is purposefully linked to my regard for others, for myself, and for life.

As I learn to anchor my intention in love, and strive to express my own highest purpose, I remind myself that others, too, are doing the best they can from where they are at each particular moment. They are working through the same maze, but they started at a different point, so they have a different route to take—no better, no worse, just different.

As I strive to understand and to progress, I find ways to transcend my insecurities through love for others, for myself, and for life. I learn to free myself from the burden of judging others and myself. I realize that unconditional acceptance and love of others—and of myself—guide my thoughts, my words, and my actions to a higher level of experience. I see that fearing the success of others is directly related to fearing my own failure. I understand, more than ever, that to be grateful for the prosperity of another is to enjoy a personal sense of peace.

As I reach toward my own aspirations, I notice others who are responsibly and tirelessly pursuing theirs as well. I detect an extraordinary force urging them to persevere, and I am reminded to be attentive to that same force within myself. I see that my very purpose is rooted in remembering my spiritual essence and in responding to my own creative impulse.

I believe that as we each hold on to a fresh sense of our spirituality, we will become more aware of a shared consciousness, and will gain a greater appreciation for the interconnection of life. We will be inclined to act more responsibly in our intentions, and it will become ever more plain that we are each a link in the circuitry of creative purpose.

As we contemplate our own creative purpose, we will attune our thought naturally to God. We will see that by honoring inspiration through expression, and offering it with love, each of us serves a unique function. We will recognize that each of us has our own spiritual paths to pursue, our own metaphysical concepts to consider, our own forms of expression to explore, and our own special insight that will help light the way for others.

Sparks of ideas will continue to come to you as you blaze your spiritual trail. Listen to them, write them down, and share them with others. Equipped with a healthy desire for discernment, invite illuminating ideas to break the obsolete boundaries of your thought.

As you encounter others who are discovering their spirituality and sharing their perceptions, consider their concepts and appreciate the exchange—but remember, always, to listen directly to God's voice.

Some might be more consciously aware of their spirituality than you are, and will even be able to teach you much about your own spirituality. But you, too, can listen, learn, progress, demonstrate your understanding, and teach others.

I will venture on, with the knowledge that as I gain a clearer, more conscious awareness of my spirituality, and practice as well as proclaim my understanding, I will learn to trust and respect my spiritual convictions—because no one is more spiritual, no one is closer to God, than I am.

And no one is more spiritual, no one is closer to God, than *you* are.

Acknowledgments

Acknowledgments

There are truly so many who have touched my life, and who have helped lead me to this place and time.

First, thank you to Modesto, California, my Central Valley roots—and, later, to Camp Verdant Vales, Verdant Vales School, and Meridian West High School—for the firm foundation and wonderfully fond growing-up memories.

Thank you to all my teachers, particularly those who regarded every single student with love, respect, and great expectation.

Thank you to UCLA for the exceptional opportunity of an unparalleled education—and for introducing me to my future husband.

Thanks to friends and colleagues in Santa Cruz, California, and to Shakespeare Santa Cruz. You are still our West Coast home.

Thanks to our Indianapolis family—an ever-expanding circle of friends in a welcoming community and truly special city. Thanks to the Indiana Repertory Theatre for bringing my husband (and thus me) here—and to the Central Indiana Community Foundation for keeping us here.

Thanks to J. B. Bowen IV for asking me to write your memoirs—what a special project that was, and what a lovely man you are.

Thanks to Michael O'Brien and Printing Partners for your generosity of time, talent, service, and spirit.

Thanks to Butler University students, faculty, and staff for welcoming me as part of your intimate and exciting theatre department. My heartfelt appreciation to both Dr. John Green and Steven Stolen for your instinctive confidence in me as a teacher.

Thanks to Lou Harry for generously sending my manuscript to your agent. Thank you, Jeremy Solomon, of First Books, for seeing something special in it.

Thanks to the Maui Writers Conference for providing a uniquely encouraging environment for writers, and for the opportunity to meet Cynthia Black and Richard Cohn of

Beyond Words Publishing. Thanks to my Ya-Ya Sisters of the Maui Writers Conference for being such a fun, supportive group.

Thanks to Beyond Words Publishing for your mission to "Inspire to Integrity," and for an ideal publishing experience. And to President and Editor-in-Chief Cynthia Black for knowing immediately that you were interested in this book. Thanks to Editor Jenefer Angell for your enthusiasm as well as your thoughtful guidance and expertise. Thanks to Julie Steigerwaldt, Adrianna Sloan, Sylvia Hayse, David Abel, Dorral Lucas, Susan Zucker, Bill Brunson, and Publishers Group West—and to everyone at Beyond Words who helped guide this book through the publishing process.

Thanks to my husband's oldest, closest friends, who have become some of my oldest, closest, and most treasured friends, too: Robert Burge (and Martha Tijerina), Paul Ecoffey, Neil Evans (and Carol DeFrancesco), and Brent Pierson (and Jillian Pierson).

Thanks to Michelle Kenzler, Barbara McKenna, Marilyn James, Ed and Susan Hutton, Audrey Stanley, Alphons Van Adrichem, Alison Trinkl, and Kathleen Becket (and so many more)—all dear friends who have maintained your friendship with my husband and me regardless of the miles between.

Thank you to my two forever friends and sisters-in-spirit, Marie Bishop and Ruthie Vandercook, for the nurturing bond and certain spark we have always shared. Thanks, also, for reading an early draft of the manuscript and offering your invaluable insight.

Thanks to everyone who read the manuscript and encouraged me.

Thanks to my sisters Carolyn Berry and Brenda Pfitzer for looking after me when I was little, and for your unconditional love ever since—and to my sister- and brother-in-law, Kelley Hunt and Gary Payne, for welcoming me into your family. And to your spouses and children for extending the family, and love, even further. Thanks to all of our combined aunts, uncles, and cousins as well.

Thanks to my dad, Jim Martin. I'm glad I took the opportunity to get to know you (thank you for offering it).

Thanks to my mother, Gretelle Martin, grandmother Marion Goodner, mother-in-law Barbara Payne, and step-mother Virginia Moore, for being amazing examples of love, strength, womanhood, and what it means to be a great mom.

Thanks to Russell Shoemake, Frank and Susie Bishop, Ima Johnson, and Jerry Cain for your loyal and lasting friendship with my mom. Your love and care were of immeasurable value to her, and to her daughters.

Thanks to my father-in-law, Chuck Payne, for being a wonderful role model as both a father and a husband. Thanks to both you and Barb for being an exemplary couple—your remarkable marriage set such a beautiful standard.

A special thank you to my church and its family. And to Timothy MacDonald, C.S.B., for your loving guidance as I continue to gain a clearer understanding.

And finally, my deepest gratitude to the love of my life, Brian Payne. Your constancy of love and support every step of the way has meant the world to me. And to the love of our life, Sweet "Baby" Jack. You seem to be propelled by joy. Brian and Jack, you both are so sweet, so special, so *genuine*—and I am so fortunate. Thank you.